Picture-Taking for Moms and Dads

Recipes for Great Pictures with Any Camera

Ron Nichols

AMHERST MEDIA, INC. ■ BUFFALO, NY

Published by:
Amherst Media, Inc.
P.O. Box 586
Buffalo, N.Y. 14226
Fax: 716-874-4508
www.AmherstMedia.com

Publisher: Craig Alesse
Senior Editor/Production Manager: Michelle Perkins
Assistant Editor: Barbara A. Lynch-Johnt
Editorial Assistant: Donna Longenecker

ISBN: 1-58428-051-4
Library of Congress Card Catalog Number: 00 135906

Printed in Korea.
10 9 8 7 6 5 4 3 2

Introduction

ACKNOWLEDGEMENTS

The trouble with saying thank you to all of the people who have had a hand in helping make my career—and this book—possible is that I'll inevitably overlook someone. Many wonderful people have helped me along on my journey. Below is a list of just a few who were especially helpful.

To my mom and dad, for making me possible. For love, patience, and support in all of my pursuits.

To Bill Dorrance, for loaning me my first camera. For expecting success. You have left this world, but your kindness lives on, my friend.

To Mr. House, high school photography teacher. For encouragement.

To Art Terry, basic press photography instructor at the University of Missouri. For helping me develop my photographic skills.

To Angus McDougal, photojournalism professor at the University of Missouri. For expecting nothing less than my best…and getting it.

To Joe Link, former editor at that little daily newspaper in Missouri. For giving me my first job and a guiding hand.

To Jon Chandler, author, performer, and songwriter extraordinaire. For helping me believe I could do this.

To Craig Alesse, publisher, photographer, and teacher. For this opportunity.

To editors Michelle Perkins and Barbara A. Lynch-Johnt. For their talents and skills in editing and packaging this book.

To all of those who have been, and will be, in my pictures. Thank you.

And finally, to my wife Betsy and my daughter Katie. For love and support and even more support. And for their patience when I said just one more picture! Even though they certainly knew it would be more than just one more.

Introduction

*O*F THE HUNDREDS OF UNIVERSITY STUDENTS who have taken my basic photography classes during the past ten years, I have a special place in my heart for those who also happen to be moms and dads. Perhaps because they are extremely motivated to capture those fleeting moments in their children's lives, or perhaps because they have a strong sense of purpose in documenting their family's history on film, the "mom and dad" photography students are consistently among the best in the class.

I thoroughly enjoy helping those young moms and dads develop the photographic skills necessary to capture images in the lives of their children and families—the special moments that will come to make up their family's visual history—moments that will be stored in scrapbooks or placed in picture frames and cherished by generations to come. I am pleased to see the look of joy and satisfaction on my students' faces when they capture those once in a lifetime moments in the lives of their children and families, or when they make a beautiful portrait of a friend. In short, I enjoy helping those students

HINTS & TIPS

Anyone can take a picture by simply loading film into the camera and snapping the shutter. Successful photographers, however, understand that there is more to taking valuable, memorable pictures than simply pushing a button. My personal goal is to teach you the techniques that will transform your casual snapshots into memorable photographs that will become treasured heirlooms.

make the transition from snapshooters to thoughtful photographers.

I've written *Picture-Taking for Moms and Dads* because I want to share those classroom lessons; I want to share the joy of creating wonderful images with moms and dads everywhere. I have incorporated nearly two decades of my experience as a photojournalist, university instructor, and a "dad" photographer into the pages that follow. Although this book is by no means a substitute for an intensive beginning photography class, it contains the core lessons and photographic illustrations that, when studied and put into practice, will help make you a better photographer.

Perhaps more importantly, *Picture-Taking for Moms and Dads* will help you capture and more thoroughly enjoy the moments that make up the life and times of your family.

Life's special occasions are memories waiting to be captured on film. Teaching moms and dads how to turn those situations into beautiful photographs is the purpose of this book. Here, a graduate mom and her graduate-to-be son share a quiet moment after a college commencement ceremony.

Children grow up all too quickly. The events not captured on film will fade away.

Cherish every moment. Enjoy creating your own rich visual history.

—*Ron Nichols*

1

Tools of the Trade

Choosing a

Camera and Film

That Are Right

for You

*A*MONG THE MOST FREQUENTLY ASKED questions I field each semester from my university students, which camera to buy is always at or near the top of the list. It's a good question, and one that almost every photographer must grapple with. It's not, however, a question that can be answered by anyone but the person who'll be using the camera. The reason? *Cameras don't take pictures, people take pictures*— cameras are simply tools for creating those pictures. The key to finding a camera that's right for you is in finding a camera that feels natural, and fits your personal and technical needs.

Cameras don't take pictures, people take pictures.

Cameras, like cars, come in all shapes, sizes, and costs. Like cars, you can get economy models with limited features, or you can get luxury models with many special features. As a working photojournalist, I need cameras and lenses that are rugged and that give me maximum creative control in taking pictures. But as an on-the-go dad, I like the features of a smaller compact camera that I can put right in my pocket so it is readily available for me when a great opportunity arises.

If you desire maximum creative control, you'll probably want to invest in a 35mm camera with manual exposure and focusing controls. If you're intimidated by the thought of manually adjusting your camera's exposure and focusing controls, an "auto-everything" 35mm camera will suit your needs.

You'll obviously purchase a camera that's within your budget. If you can afford it, it's a good idea to get a camera that has a built-in flash and a zoom lens. Make sure

OPPOSITE: Simple point and shoot cameras provide consistent results under most conditions. But if you want more creative control (like choosing a slow shutter speed to record the movement of water seen here) you'll want to purchase a camera that gives you advanced exposure control options. Once you've made such a purchase, enroll in a basic photography class at a local community college to master advanced photographic techniques.

that whatever camera you're considering fits your "technical comfort zone," too. In other words, make sure you're comfortable with its use and operation before you buy.

It's always best to thoroughly research several cameras before you make a purchase. A camera is an investment that should last for years. If you have lots of photographic experience, you may already know what special features you'd like in your next camera. But if you're just getting started, you may want to ask other moms and dads which cameras they use and why. You might also want to ask the sales representatives at several local camera stores about various cameras and their features. Photography magazines and Internet web sites also provide a wealth of information regarding cameras, features, and prices.

Although there are many models, brands, and features from which to choose, there are four major groups of cameras.

Choosing a Camera

POINT AND SHOOT CAMERAS. Sometimes referred to as lens shutter cameras, point and shoot cameras are compact, easy to use 35mm and Advanced Photo System (APS) cameras. They generally feature automatic exposure control and automatic focus so you can just "point and shoot" when taking a picture. Because they are so compact, easy to use, and often feature zoom lenses (see illustrations), they are ideal for on-the-go moms and dads. And because they are automated, they render acceptable photographs in most situations. They don't provide the creative exposure and focus control that single lens reflex cameras do, however.

Point and shoot (compact) cameras feature automatic exposure and focusing features in an easy-to-carry package. (Photo courtesy of Pentax)

HINTS & TIPS

Although not likely to replace the versatile and popular 35mm format, the Advanced Photo System, with its easy-to-use features, offers amateur photographers several advantages:

■ Smaller film size allows cameras to be smaller and easier to handle

■ A leaderless, drop-in film cartridge prevents film-loading mistakes

■ Negatives are returned in the original cartridge, so there's no danger in mishandling the film. Keeping track of the negatives is also easier.

■ APS photographers can choose between three print formats (including panoramic) and can change the format at any time during the roll.

■ For ease of filing and reprinting, an index print is provided along with the processed prints, showing all of the positive images on a single print.

■ Information regarding the shooting conditions is recorded on a special magnetic track on the film. This information helps film processors render higher quality prints.

SINGLE LENS REFLEX CAMERAS. The most popular choice of camera for photojournalists and advanced amateur photographers, 35mm single lens reflex (SLR) cameras provide greater exposure control and feature interchangeable lenses, so you can shoot with a variety of lenses—from wide angle to macro to telephoto. Although SLRs are more expensive than point and shoot cameras, the SLR's ability to take new lenses allows for a greater range of shots and is a real creative advantage.

Single Lens Reflex (SLR) cameras provide greater exposure control and feature interchangeable lenses among other features. (Photo courtesy of Canon.)

Unlike point and shoot cameras, which allow you to preview an image through a window near the lens, SLR camera systems use a mirror and viewscreen that allow you to preview an image through the lens itself. Because the photographer can look through the camera's lens and see what the lens sees when taking the picture, he can compose the picture more accurately. Most SLRs also come with automatic or programmable exposure controls. Many feature automatic focus control as well.

SINGLE USE CAMERAS. Single use (disposable) cameras are inexpensive cameras that are preloaded with film. Disposable cameras are designed for general use, underwater use, or for shooting panoramic photos. Some come equipped with a built-in flash. Once you've exposed all of the film in the camera, you simply take the camera to a film processing store; your prints are returned to you, but the camera is not. Because disposable cameras are inexpensive and easy to use, they are perfect for use by guests at special functions like parties, weddings, or receptions.

DIGITAL CAMERAS. Rather than recording images on light-sensitive film, digital cameras record images in an electronic or digital format. Photos taken with a digital camera can be viewed on a computer immediately after taking them. The resulting images can be manipulated, duplicated, and transmitted electronically over the Internet to anywhere in the world.

Digital cameras offer many of the features of point and shoot cameras, but record images in an electronic format rather than on film. (Photo courtesy of Nikon)

Once you've chosen the camera and format that are right for you, heed this advice: Prior to taking your first picture, read the owner's manual for the camera from beginning to end so you're familiar with its overall operation. It details how you can use the camera's special features to help you take better photos. The owner's manual is also an invaluable source of information on the camera's care.

Camera Lenses

THE VERSATILE ZOOM. Whether you use a point and shoot, SLR, single use, or digital camera, your camera may very likely come with a zoom lens. Zoom lenses offer a variety of lenses all rolled into one. With the push of a button (for automatic zooms), you can achieve shots typically made by normal, wide angle, and

14

Many point and shoot cameras come with zoom lenses. These lenses provide multiple focal lengths (or angles of view) in one. Here, a wide angle lens (28mm) was used at a distance of about six feet. (Notice the wide angle of view and how much of the background you can see.)

In this image, a normal (50mm) lens was used; the photo was taken from the same distance as the previous photograph.

In this image, a telephoto (105mm) lens was used; the photo was taken from the same distance as the photographs above. Notice the narrow angle of view and how very little of the background you can see.

even moderate telephoto lenses. Zoom lenses reduce the time spent changing lenses, moving closer and further from your subject, and are easier to carry than a camera bag filled with lenses. A typical zoom lens for a point and shoot camera is 28–85mm. The numbers represent the focal length of the lens—the smaller the number, the wider the angle; the bigger the number, the tighter the angle. In the case of a 28–85mm zoom, the widest angle is 28mm and the tightest angle is 85mm. You can also use all of the focal lengths in between.

Zoom lenses reduce the time spent changing lenses.

THE WIDE ANGLE. When using a wide angle lens (16–40mm), objects appear further away than when viewed with the naked eye. The angle of view is also wider than is seen with the eyes focused in a fixed position. The wide angle allows you to increase the area you see when you look through your lens, and thus allows you to include more of a scene in your composition. Wide angle lenses work well for shooting scenics, group shots, and even for some portraits.

A potential drawback to using wide angle lenses, however, is distortion. Objects photographed close with a wide angle lens appear disproportionately larger than objects further away. The wider the angle of view, the greater the potential distortion. Consequently, wide angle lenses are not considered ideal for close-up portraits since they create distortion of facial features.

THE NORMAL LENS. A normal lens on a 35mm camera is 45–55mm. This angle of view approximates the perspective you achieve in fixing your eyes on a particular scene. It's the standard lens sold with SLR cameras. This lens is useful in a variety of situations, including scenics, mid-length, and full-length portraits.

THE TELEPHOTO LENS. These lenses, which feature focal lengths greater than 55mm, are especially useful for mid-length and head and shoulders portraits, sports, candids, and some scenics. Telephoto lenses also yield images that seem to have been taken at a closer range, allowing you to get "closer" to scenes when you can't walk there.

Telephoto lenses cover less background area than "normal" lenses. This simplifies and improves most portraits by eliminating distracting background clutter.

Choosing Film

Film is the medium upon which your photographic images are made. Since light is the catalyst in capturing an image on film, the amount of light that is allowed to hit the film is very important. Properly exposed film will result in photographs that are neither too dark nor too light. Producing properly exposed images is, of course, your goal.

HINTS & TIPS

Start with ASA 400 film. Then, experiment with other film speeds to discover what you personally like or dislike about each one.

Film speed ratings (ASA or ISO numbers) tell your camera how much light must hit the film in order to make a properly exposed image. The higher the number of the film's rating (ASA or ISO), the more sensitive the film is to light. In other words, a film with an ASA of 400 is twice as sensitive to light as ASA 200 film, so only half as much light is needed to make an exposure of the same scene.

  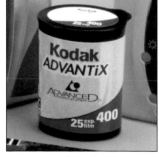

LEFT TO RIGHT: Color print film (color negative), color transparency (slide) film, and APS film are available from several manufacturers, and comes in a range of film speeds to fit almost any situation.

There's an inverse relationship between film speed and the amount of light that's required for proper exposure: the higher the speed, the less light needed to take a properly exposed photograph. Higher-speed films tend to produce more grain on the final prints or slides. The larger the grain, the lower your photo's resolution. However, unless you're enlarging photographs to more than 8"x10", this shouldn't be a problem. (For larger prints (11"x14" to 16"x20"), a slower speed film (i.e., ISO 100) will provide the best results.) ASA 400 film will likely be your best bet in almost any situation (with the exception of big enlargements).

COLOR PRINT FILM. For most at-home applications, color print film will be the film of choice. As discussed earlier, when picking a color print film for most applications, you'll probably want to choose a film with an ASA/ISO rating of 400. Kodak Royal Gold 400 and Fujicolor 400 are two excellent films.

Because color film is so widely used today, choosing to use black & white film can help make a photograph truly unique. Custom photo labs can print your black & white images on archival paper that can last for hundreds of years in scrapbooks or in frames.

HINTS & TIPS

Because few commercial photo labs offer traditional black & white processing, several manufacturers offer black & white film that can be developed with a color film process called C-41. This film (like Ilford's XP-2) gives photographers the opportunity to take black & white photos, even if they do not have access to more expensive custom labs. The film also has finer grain characteristics than standard black & white film, and therefore yields beautiful enlargements. Negatives from C-41–processed black & white film can also be printed at custom labs to yield sepia or brown-toned photos.

COLOR TRANSPARENCY FILM. If you enjoy putting together slide shows, color transparency will be the film for you. Slides are also easier to file and catalog than prints.

BLACK & WHITE FILM. If you're looking for variety, or perhaps a photo to accompany some old black & white prints, try shooting black & white film. For the best results, have your final images printed at a lab that specializes in black & white custom prints. You can have these prints toned and can even handcolor your black & white photos for a unique image.

Custom photo labs can also add a sepia tone to your black & white print for an antiquated look or to match pictures from previous generations.

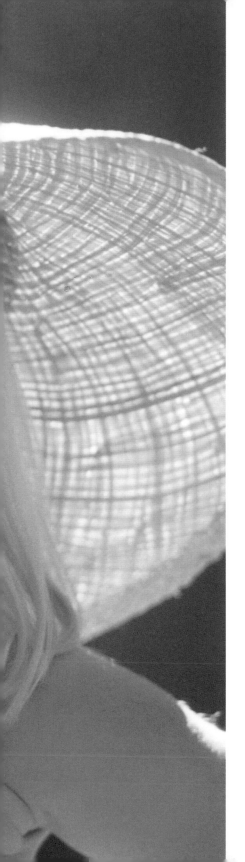

2

Better Pictures— Now!

Five Easy Steps

to Shooting

Like a Pro

*L*EARNING TO SHOOT GREAT PHOTOGRAPHS, like learning any new skill, takes time, patience, practice, commitment, and sometimes luck. Fortunately, by utilizing five simple techniques, you can add instant impact and professional style to your photographs.

The trick is learning to see. Anyone who's ever tried it knows there's no such thing as a quick walk around the block with a three year old. Children at that age are constantly stopping to explore, touch, and sometimes taste the world around them. Sticks, cans, rocks, feathers, leaves, flowers, and almost every other conceivable item are riches in the eyes of a child—treasures that must be explored, and sometimes even taken home.

Children are constantly stopping to explore.

Unfortunately, for most adults, the phrase "if you've seen it once, you've seen it a hundred times" has become a mantra that truly represents the degree to which we have become visually desensitized to the world around us. We take pictures that reflect this limited perspective and, not surprisingly, our picture-taking has suffered for it.

Angle of View

Most photographs are taken from a height of 5–6 feet—roughly the height of the average adult. It seems logical to shoot from this vantage point, doesn't it? After all, shouldn't we seek to create images that mirror the perspective from which we typically view life—the way we're used to seeing things?

However, by simply changing your perspective, taking a photograph from a lower or higher angle, you can transform the ordinary into extraordinary. In changing

OPPOSITE: Shooting from a high angle (looking down upon the scene) can create a unique perspective and eliminate distracting colors or objects in the background. This can be especially helpful in composing portraits.

Sometimes, a close-up can provide a unique view of the world. Here, well-worn ballet shoes, photographed from floor level, tell of a ballerina's hard work and dedication.

your perspective, you will change the way you see the world and, most importantly, you'll change the way the world sees your photographs. In other words, you can add visual interest in your photographs by simply seeking a perspective that most picture-takers won't take the time to explore. A unique angle will often yield a unique photograph.

Consider it Playtime

During playtime with your child, you have probably gotten down on his or her level. If you're going to photograph a child, it's often best to do the same. Not only do you provide a unique perspective for those who see

HINTS & TIPS

your photos, but by photographing a child from his or her perspective, you also help convey the world through his or her eyes. By photographing a crawling child from floor level, you'll see the world as your child does—uniquely.

A change in perspective can also help eliminate distracting backgrounds. Shooting from a unique angle might offer protection against distracting, unattractive

A change in perspective can make an ordinary image look very unique and eliminate distracting backgrounds.

telephone poles or other obstacles that might adversely affect your photograph. Of course, there are no set rules for shooting from unusual perspectives. Good photographers are always on the lookout for the perspective that will most effectively present the visual information they want to convey.

Photographers should explore their world.

Like the three-year-old child who constantly explores his or her world, photographers should explore their world, seeking a new vision and looking for opportunities to record that vision in a new or interesting way. Learning to see like a child again will not only yield better photographs for you and your family, it will invariably yield a heightened sense of visual awareness and pleasure in your day-to-day life. How's that for an incentive?

Get Close

By far, the biggest mistake made by most beginning photography students is shooting their pictures too far away from their subjects. I urge (rather, implore) beginning students to get closer to their subjects. One way to make sure you're close enough is to fill the viewfinder with only the most important visual information before snapping the shutter. By simply getting closer, certain visual distractions (i.e., trees, power lines, telephone poles, etc.) in the photograph are eliminated. If you can't physically get close to your subject, use a telephoto lens. Regardless of your method, closer is almost always better.

Perhaps the best philosophy in composing a picture is waste not, want not. Think of photographs as containing precious space. Don't waste that space on unimportant or distracting elements. If you follow my advice and fill the viewfinder with only the most important information before you shoot, your photographs will

Many photographs lack impact because the subject was too far away when the photograph was taken—making it difficult to see what's happening in the scene. In the first photo (top), the subject blends in with the background, and the overall scene is confusing. Moving closer to the subject, and filling the viewfinder with as much of the main subject as possible makes a better photograph. In the second photo (bottom), we clearly see what the subject is doing, and the distracting background clutter is eliminated.

have much more impact. Plus, by getting close, the subject of the photograph becomes obvious—especially to those who see your images in scrapbooks or in picture frames.

One brief technical note—while closer is usually better, you need to be aware that there is a limit to how close your particular camera can focus. Most point and shoot cameras (those that do not require manual focusing or light controls) have a minimum focusing distance of 2–3 feet. If you shoot an image closer than that, it will not be in focus. Be sure to read the camera's manual to see how close you can get with your camera.

Don't Hit the Bull's-Eye

To create impact in their photographs, photographers arrange objects in a manner that creates order and increases visual interest. The process of arranging the elements in a scene is called composition. Well-composed photographs provide a clear focal point, a point of visual interest that results in a photograph that is both easy and pleasant to view.

Arranging the elements in a scene is called composition.

In viewing a well-composed photograph, the eye takes in the many elements of a composition with ease. It's the photographer's job to decide what elements will be in the photograph, and how those elements should be arranged. Practically speaking, this means the photographer will determine how close to get to the subject and what angle or perspective would best suit the composition.

One surefire way to create good composition in your photographs is to avoid placing the subject in the center of the frame. Beginning photographers need t

OPPOSITE, TOP: *Placing the subject in the center (or bull's-eye) of the frame creates a static image.*
OPPOSITE, BOTTOM: *The composition of this photograph is improved by positioning the camera so the subject is placed in the scene using the rule of thirds.*

work hard to avoid the bull's-eye effect. Focusing aids and light meters in cameras are placed in the center of the camera's viewfinder, so many people incorrectly assume that's where they should place the subject.

To create visually pleasing images, try using a compositional technique called the rule of thirds. When used properly, it can guide you in subject placement—you'll never fall prey to the dreaded bull's-eye effect again! Looking through the viewfinder, imagine that the camera's frame is divided into equal thirds, both vertically and horizontally—sort of like an elongated tic-tac-toe grid. Try to place your subject away from the center, and near one of the quadrant intersections.

The rule of thirds is also helpful when photographing a landscape in which the horizon is a composition-

Shooting into a mirror can create a very interesting image. In the original photograph (right), the composition wasn't quite right, though. Cropping the photo improved it dramatically (above), and removed some of the distracting elements in the background.

al element. Whether you're shooting a horizontal image or a vertical one, avoid dividing the picture in half with the horizon line. Instead, place the horizon in either the top third or lower third of the frame. This will significantly improve the composition, adding impact and interest to your pictures.

There are no hard and fast rules in photography. Although I recommend avoiding the bull's-eye effect, some centered subjects work well compositionally. In general, though, by using the rule of thirds, you will improve the results of your photographic efforts.

There are no hard and fast rules in photography.

Keep in mind, if your photographic composition wasn't exactly what you wanted when you initially made the original photograph, a custom photo lab can "crop" (or resize) the photograph. Often, photographs can simply be trimmed to enhance the composition.

Slow Down, Shoot More

In the hustle and bustle of today's lifestyles, many of us find it difficult to slow down. Learning to slow down, however, is precisely what you need to do to improve your photographs, and perhaps your appreciation of the world around you, as well.

"Good seeing" is the key to good photography, and good seeing requires good footwork. In order to shoot from unique perspectives, capture the right light, and properly frame your subjects, you'll need to use your feet to get there. Once in position, take the time to "soak it all in," and decide what angle or perspective will make the best picture(s).

Most amateur photographers simply "grab" pictures in a moment's haste. Successful photographers know there's no point to shooting the photo until it's properly composed. Before taking the photograph, really explore your subject; look at it from different angles. Observe from above, below, and from various sides; see the world through your viewfinder, then ask yourself, which of the possible angles will make the best picture?

After you've slowly and thoughtfully composed the scene, wait for the right moment to take the photograph. Sometimes that means waiting for the right light, the right expression, or the right action. In many scenes—particularly those with children and family—*when* you take the picture actually determines the quality of the picture. A surprised expression after opening a gift, arms raised in victory after scoring a soccer goal, or a child's tear-filled eyes after a first haircut could yield some pretty spectacular photographs.

Achieving the right feel for your photograph is worth the wait.

When the right moment finally comes along, shoot several frames. Carefully considered compositions are the mark of a successful photographer, and when you slow down and capture the feel of the moment, you'll preserve cherished memories (not to mention beautiful photos). With the "slow down, shoot more" approach, you're guaranteed to achieve a more professional look.

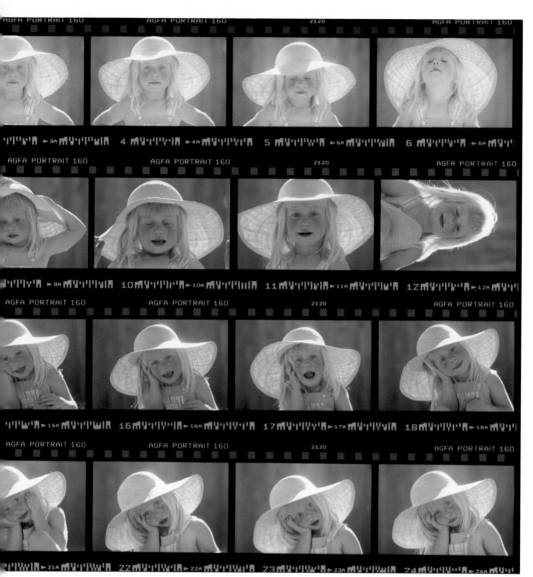

Take the lead from professional photographers. Once you've carefully composed the scene, photograph the subject as the situation unfolds. Children will often offer up a variety of captivating facial expressions and actions within a short period of time.

3

The Right Light

Seeing the Best Light for Better Pictures

Photography is all about light. Recording that light on film makes photographs possible. Seeing and recording the best light on film (and also knowing what times of day to avoid) is central to making great photographs.

The Golden Hours

With the exception of overcast days, the best times of day to take photos are from sunrise until about an hour after sunrise, and from about an hour before sunset through sunset. These times of day are often called the golden hours because of the warm, soft, golden light created by the sun. Skin tones look great in this

BELOW: Golden hour light is unsurpassed in capturing natural beauty.
OPPOSITE: The golden hours provide the perfect light for making pictures of people. Skin tones are made warm and soft, and there are no harsh shadows in the eyes of the subject.

light; in fact, all colors in the scene are enhanced by this beautiful natural light.

Not surprisingly, the golden hours are not always the most convenient times to shoot. But for beautiful scenics and gorgeous portraits, the light truly is worth the wait.

Overcast Days

Overcast days create a soft, indirect light that is excellent for taking photographs. In the past, it was advised to avoid shooting on cloudy days. This was due, in large part, to the combination of slower film speeds and fixed exposure settings of yesteryear's cameras. But thanks to faster film and cameras with adjustable exposure controls, shooting on overcast days is not only pos-

The overall tone of photographs taken on overcast days is soft and even, without deep shadows or areas of bright highlights. Some cameras offer a "fill-flash" option. This adds just enough light to brighten a photo without overpowering the subject.

sible, it's desirable, especially for portraits and even some scenics.

Like the light during the golden hours, overcast light produces no harsh shadows with which to contend. Additionally, the color saturation (or intensity) of the film is increased, making the colors in your prints and slides look richer.

Indoors

Indoor photography often requires a flash. Using a faster speed film (ISO 400 or higher) can record many situations even without a flash.

Many of the situations that you'll want to photograph will be composed indoors. If there's not enough light and you're using an automatic camera, a flash may be activated in order to create a proper exposure—especially if you're using slower film speeds. But because the light comes directly from the camera, the flash can

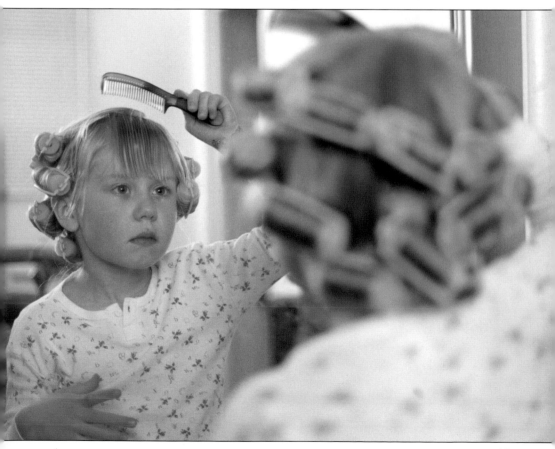

HINTS & TIPS

Red-eye occurs when the light from your camera's flash bounces directly off the rods and cones on the back wall of the subject's eyes, giving the eyes a red, glowing appearance in the final prints.

One way to reduce red-eye is to lighten the room as much as possible. This will cause the pupils of the subject's eyes to constrict, and will reduce the area of potential reflectance. Cameras with built-in red-eye reduction provide a series of pre-exposure light emissions that create the same effect. The bursts of light cause the pupils in the eyes to constrict, thereby reducing the potential for red-eye.

If neither of these options are available, try having the subject turn his/her head at an angle to the camera to prevent the flash from having a direct line to the back of the eyes.

---

cause red-eye and undesirable background shadows. You'll find that there are just some situations that require indoor lighting. If possible, though, try moving your subject away from nearby walls to avoid the background shadows created by the flash.

> There are just some situations that require indoor lighting.

It is important to note that, because most film is designed to be used in outdoor conditions or with a flash, shooting indoors under incandescent or florescent lights will cause the colors in your final prints to shift or change hues. Incandescent lights will cause a yellow color cast, while fluorescent lights will cause a green one. If you'll be shooting color images under indoor light, using print film (rather than slide film) is advantageous because most color labs can color-correct your final prints. Because black & white film renders colors in tones of neutral gray, it can be used effectively and without color shifts in any light.

OPPOSITE: Backlit subjects, like these empty bottles, can make beautiful photographs for decorating either the home or office.

Window Light

Window light provides perfect light for some photographs. Soft light from a window can be a beautiful source for portraits, especially on overcast days. When photographing a subject using window light, be certain the light falls on half to three-quarters of the subject's face.

Avoid Midday Light

It makes sense that if the first and the last light of the day are the best times to shoot photographs, then one should avoid taking pictures in the middle of the day in bright sunlight. Midday light creates less than appealing skin tones, mutes colors, and creates harsh shadows on faces.

If possible, avoid shooting at mid-day. The light is harsh and is often uncomfortable for the subject (above). If you must shoot at mid-day, try moving your subject into a shaded area (right).

4

Creating Treasured Memories

Techniques for Beautiful Portraits

O F ALL PHOTOGRAPHS, portraits are, by far, the most numerous. Portraits often adorn the desks or walls in offices throughout the world. The majority of us carry a portrait or two of family members in our wallets, so we can always have our loved ones close by.

Simple Portraits

Although formal studio portraits can be beautiful, there's nothing like natural, casual portraits of our friends and family.

Good portraits incorporate all the photographic tips discussed in the previous chapters. Getting close, using good composition, and choosing the right light are the perfect ingredients in the recipe for beautiful portraits. By following a few additional tips, the portraits you create will have a unique and professional look.

LENS. By using a telephoto lens to take your portraits, you can get close to the subject without getting too close for your subject's comfort. Telephoto lenses are also ideal for portraits because they do not cause wide angle distortion, and they reduce background clarity.

Telephoto lenses are ideal for portraits because they do not distort facial features like wide-angle lenses (see chapter 1). When used "up close" telephoto lenses all but eliminate distracting elements and clutter in the background. The use of a telephoto lens simplifies your portrait, drawing more attention to the subject, thereby making the photo more effective.

FOCUS. For a portrait to be successful, the eyes of the subject must be sharp and in focus. Whether you use a camera with auto focus, or one with manual focus,

> There's nothing like natural, casual portraits.

always be certain to focus critically on the eyes of your subject.

BACKGROUND. When setting up a portrait, pick a simple, nondistracting background and avoid putting your subject up against a wall (like a police mug shot!). When shooting a simple portrait, backgrounds should be "seen but not heard." In other words, they shouldn't overwhelm the subject, but rather, should provide a pleasant backdrop for the subject. When it comes to casual portraits, keep the background soft and simple.

Getting close to the subject reduces depth of field (or the focusing depth of a picture), which helps eliminate almost all distractions in the background.

HINTS & TIPS

Here are some additional suggestions for keeping the background in your photos simple:

■ When setting up your portraits, avoid walls and backgrounds with strong lines or distracting colors.

■ Whenever possible, try to move your subject as far away from walls as possible.

■ Shoot with a telephoto lens and fill up the frame with as much of your subject as possible—there's little chance that you'll have a busy background if your subject is blocking it from view.

LOCATION. There are limitless opportunities for you to create great portraits. You can make a portrait that "fits" your subject's personality and interests at almost any location. Many people love nature, so composing a portrait of a nature lover outdoors makes sense. Also, because of the individualized environment, it's likely that your portrait will be as unique as your subject.

COMFORT. The photographer's greatest challenge can often be getting the subject to relax and to look comfortable. That's why moms and dads can be such good portrait photographers. Their subjects (other friends and family members) know and trust the photographer, so the level of anxiety is greatly reduced. Picking a comfortable environment also helps a subject relax.

POSING. Some subjects might look to you, as the photographer, for directions on how they should pose. The best pose for portraits, however, is one that the subject falls into naturally, and most people will find that comfortable and natural pose when allowed to get comfortable on their own. You may occasionally need to prompt them to assume a natural pose with a well-timed suggestion or two.

OPPOSITE: Instead of trying to "direct" a pose, ask the subject to find a pose that is comfortable. The subject will be happier, and the photograph will have a more natural look.

There are limitless opportunities for you to create great portraits.

50

HINTS & TIPS

Here are a few additional suggestions to help with posing your subject:

■ Have your subject cross his/her arms while leaning comfortably against a fence or tree.

■ If seated or reclining, have your subject rest his/her chin in the hands.

■ A slight head tilt or head turn can provide a more relaxed and photogenic look.

■ Whether standing, sitting or reclining, the pose should reflect good body posture.

■ Generally, your subject should look into the camera, so in the final photo, your subject will make eye contact with those who view the photograph.

■ Try to shoot at eye-level or above for a more flattering viewpoint.

LIGHT. Again, try to shoot your portraits at a time of day that takes advantage of the golden hour, shoot on an overcast day, or in a shaded area on bright days. Those lighting conditions will yield better colors, less contrast, and favorable skin tones. In addition, the subject is less likely to squint.

By reducing contrast in the scene (or situations containing bright areas and very dark or shaded areas in the same photograph) you'll eliminate those deep shadows in the eyes of your subject and your photograph will have more pleasant, even tones throughout.

STYLE. There's no doubt that getting closer improves photographs. In making portraits, how close you get depends on whether you want a tight head-and-shoulders portrait, a mid-length portrait, or a full-length portrait. Though you prefer a specific style of pose, it might be a good idea to shoot several frames of each of the three. You can always decide which one you prefer later.

EYES. For most portraits, you should have the subject look directly at the camera. People like to feel that they can look a subject in the eye when viewing a photo. This is why many magazine covers feature portraits with direct eye

OPPOSITE: Don't forget that portraits can be head and shoulders, mid-length, or full-length, as seen here.

There's no doubt that getting closer improves photographs.

Using direct flash (right) can create shadows on walls and the dreaded red-eye effect. By moving your subjects near a natural light source (in the case of the image below, an open door), the need to use direct flash is eliminated, creating a more natural look.

contact. It's an honest and direct approach. Plus, there's nothing like looking into the eyes of friends and loved ones, even when it's just a picture.

Pet Portraits

There's no doubt that pets are important members of our families. Pet portraits make ɑluable additions to scrapbooks and look great in picture frames. Making a pet portrait is not unlike making people portraits. The best pet portraits also feature the basic composition and lighting principles noted earlier.

Depending on the personality (and tolerance) of the pet, props can be used to create special seasonal pictures.

OPPOSITE: Pets are special members of our families. The same basic "people portrait" techniques can also be used to take keepsake portraits of our four-legged friends.

Some pets are infinitely more cooperative than their human counterparts (especially when offered a treat or two), but pets do pose certain portrait challenges. For example, you'll likely need help keeping the pet's attention while taking the picture. Pets that are easily distracted can challenge even the most patient photographer, so don't get discouraged if all of your hard work runs off before you get a chance to make your picture. If unsuccessful with a "posed" portrait, keep your camera nearby and be ready for a candid pet portrait.

Environmental Portraits

Simple portraits show us what a person looks like and the good ones sometimes provide insight about the

Because they feature elements from the world around the subject, environmental portraits tell us something about that person's hobbies, interests, or occupation.

subject's personality. Another kind of portrait, an environmental portrait, shows us more than just the subject, it helps us understand the subject's occupation, interests, or hobbies.

Environmental portraits should include enough of the subject's environment to tell us about the subject. A firefighter in a fire station, gardeners in their gardens, a pilot in the cockpit of the airplane, and a teacher surrounded by her students in a classroom are all examples of environmental portraits.

Ensure that the subject is the prominent feature in the photograph.

The key to shooting successful environmental portraits is to ensure that the subject is the prominent feature in the photograph. Be sure to compose the shot with enough "relevant" environmental information to reflect the subject's occupation or interests.

Props

Sometimes having the subject hold or stand near an important object makes a wonderful image. A child holding an art masterpiece or a craft project, a Girl Scout holding several boxes of cookies, or a child holding a little puppy are all examples of props.

Again, the basic portrait-taking principles apply. Get close, use good light, and pick an appropriate background. Place the subject and the object close together. This way, there is no wasted space in the frame, and both the subject and the object will be in focus.

OPPOSITE: *Whether it's a special project, or a special friend, having your subject hold an object when making the portrait can add interest to the shot.*

5

Picture-Perfect Vacations

How to Shoot

Spectacular

Scenics

T here's nothing like a vacation. For your children, it may be the highlight of their year. Seeing new landscapes, experiencing new events, and meeting new people are all part of the vacation experience.

At most vacation sites, you'll have the opportunity to purchase a postcard featuring a professionally photographed scene. But shooting your own photos is much more personal and certainly more satisfying.

Beautiful images make very special, personal gifts for family and friends.

The well-composed, well-lit scenic images that you create can later be enlarged, matted, and framed to decorate your home or office. Again, there's immense satisfaction in knowing that you made the images that are on display in your own home. Also, beautiful images make very special, personal gifts for family and friends.

Since we all tend to tire of our own surroundings, taking pictures while on vacation can be a refreshing change of pace. With new landscapes to see and photograph, you'll feel inspired to create memorable photos to frame and fill your scrapbooks. By using the techniques for composition, lighting, and portraiture found in the previous chapters, you'll be on the road to doing just that. If you're the competitive type, you may also want to consider submitting those fantastic photos to a few local photography contests that feature prizes for vacation photos, and other categories, as well.

Tips for Scenics

The following suggestions will also help you to dramatically improve your vacation photos:

FRAMING. Look for opportunities to "frame" the scene. Framing helps give your scenics more depth and

OPPOSITE, TOP: A church is framed with the outline of a heart in a fence. Framing the subject gives the photograph a sense of depth and dimension.
OPPOSITE, BOTTOM: Foreground objects (like tree limbs or rocks) also give photographs depth and dimension.

HINTS & TIPS

Many vacationers arrive at their destinations by air. If you'd like to take aerial photos from your airline seat, keep these tips in mind:

■ Be sure to turn your camera's flash off.

■ Wait until the sun is behind you to take your pictures (this will reduce glare and will minimize the plexiglass scratches).

■ Keep your camera as close to the window as possible (this will reduce the amount of glare from the inside of the airplane).

---

helps provide a clear focal point for your images. Tree branches, doors, windows, flowers or other foreground objects can help frame a scene used in the composition of your photograph.

FOREGROUND OBJECTS. Look for foreground objects to place in the scene. This provides visual balance and gives your pictures more depth and visual interest. Foreground objects (or elements that are closest to you in the scene) can come in the form of flowers, rocks, water, leaves or other objects.

Look for opportunities to create panoramic scenics.

PANORAMICS. Look for opportunities to create panoramic scenics—they often make great compositions. APS cameras generally offer a panoramic function as a standard feature, but single use (disposable) panoramic cameras are available for those using a 35mm camera.

STILL LIFE. Keep an eye out for interesting still life compositions—local plants, foods, crafts, clothes and other objects can be the subject of unique and interesting vacation photos.

CLOSE-UPS. Simple close-ups of flowers or other subjects can be among the most stunning images you'll make.

ENVIRONMENTAL PORTRAITS. Make environmental portraits of your family at various points of interest.

Sunset. When you take pictures at sunset—almost anywhere—you have the backdrop for beautiful images, especially if you can find a silhouetted object to place in the scene. As well as being suitable for framing, sunsets make great closing photos for scrapbook stories and slide shows.

A dad and his son share a moment on a fishing dock at the end of the day. Sunset photographs are good closing photos for vacation slide shows, as well as scrapbooks, and memory books.

Keeping Film Safe

X-Rays. When travelling to and from your vacation destination, keeping your film safe (and all of those vacation memories) should be a primary concern. The same airport x-ray screening machines that keep you safe during your trip can damage your film. X-rays act like light on film, which can create a fog on your final images. The more often your film is exposed to x-rays, the more likely the film will be damaged. Whenever possible, do not pass your film through those machines. Instead, ask the security personnel to hand inspect your film. It will only take an extra moment or two, but it could save those wonderful vacation images.

HINTS & TIPS

To avoid camera catastrophes in tropical locations, consider the following precautions:

■ While on the beach, keep your camera in a sealed plastic bag until you're ready to use it.

■ Avoid loading or unloading film in sandy areas. When handling your camera or film, make certain your hands are clean.

■ Never leave your camera in direct sunlight or in a car parked in the sun.

TROPICAL VACATIONS. Tropical getaways offer special photographic opportunities, but also pose additional camera-handling considerations. Soaking up the rays on a warm sandy beach may be good for the soul, but sand (especially very fine sand) can wreak havoc on your camera equipment. Water and high temperatures (such as in a car that's parked in the sun) can also be extremely damaging to your equipment.

If you plan on snorkeling during your stay, several manufacturers offer "single purpose" or "disposable" underwater cameras that are convenient, easy to use, and inexpensive. Most of these cameras have an operating range of up to ten feet underwater, which is perfect for most casual photographers.

Keep your eyes open for some of nature's little surprises. Sometimes small, simple scenes can have as much, or more, beauty than breathtaking vistas.

6

Using and Displaying Photos

How to

Share and Enjoy

Your Images

By following the basic picture taking advice in this book, you'll be well on your way to shooting great photos. With time, practice and tenacity, your photographs will continue to improve and your cache of keepsake photos will swell.

But what do you do with those "prize winning" photos once you have them in your hand? This chapter explores some of the many ways you can use your photographs for fun—and maybe even a little profit.

Editing

When you get your processed film back, the first step in using your photos is to decide which ones *not* to use. When you slow down and shoot more, you'll probably end up with several frames of each scene, subject or expression. Take a tip from the pros—choose the best images and set the others aside. Look for images with good exposure, good composition and interesting subjects. Once you have your favorites, you can decide how to use them.

Enlargements

With some of your most special images, you'll probably want to have enlargements made for framing and decorating your home or office. When making enlargements, keep in mind the film speed that the image was shot on. If you used film with an ISO or ASA of 400 or more, you'll probably want to enlarge a 35mm or APS negative to no more than 8"x10". If you used a slower film, you can probably get good results with prints up to 16"x20".

> You'll probably want to have enlargements made for framing.

HINTS & TIPS

When purchasing enlargements, it is also important to keep in mind that the aspect ratio (the proportion of height to width) of your negative may be different than the aspect ratio of some print sizes. As a result, when the enlargement is made some cropping may occur. Often, this is no problem. But, if something in your photo runs close to the edge of the print and you want to make sure it doesn't get cropped off, you'll need to provide special instructions when you place your order.

If possible, take the original print, along with your negative, to the lab. If you are happy with the colors in it, let them know that you'd like the enlargement to match it as closely as possible. If the original print isn't quite right (say, you shot the picture in incandescent light and it has a yellow color cast), tell them that, too. Often, this can be corrected in a reprint or enlargement.

If you have access to a custom photo lab, you can consider having images cropped, if that will improve the composition or remove a distracting element. Cropping simply means that the lab prints only part of the negative instead of the whole.

You can also neatly trim the images yourself, using a sharp paper cutter or razor blade. You can also use scissors, but these can produce an uneven edge.

Keep in mind, when you crop or trim an image, you will more than likely end up with an image of a nonstandard size. This means you'll be less likely to find off-the-rack frames and mats to fit it.

Seasonal Cards

When it comes to making your own seasonal cards, commercial photo labs provide a variety of printing options—especially at holiday time. A family photo personalized with your holiday greeting creates a card that is sure to bring smiles to whomever receives one.

Today's color printing technology allows nearly everyone an opportunity to print attractive, inexpensive calendars. Many quick-copy vendors provide color printing services which will allow you to feature one or more of your photos on calendars and other printed materials. By using some of your own great photos on a calendar, you'll have a monthly source of pride and inspiration.

You'll have a monthly source of pride and inspiration.

If you have a photo-quality color printer, you have even more options. You can make your own mailing labels, insert your photos into letters, or print copies of your images to share.

Shirts and Mugs

The same technology that provides the means to print color photographs for personal calendars can also be applied on other novelty items. Color t-shirts, sweatshirts, coffee mugs, plates and mouse pads are all great media for displaying your photos. You'll be amazed at what wonderful conversation starters they can be!

Photo Contests

Taking great photographs is a thrill unto itself. But winning the accolades of others can be even more rewarding. From local to national, there are literally hundreds of opportunities to compete for fun and prizes. Photography magazines and newsletters sometimes provide contest opportunities, or you can ask at your local camera store about photography clubs in your area that might sponsor contests. A search of the world wide web will yield many more opportunities as well. One site (<amateurphoto.about.com>) provides a listing of a wide range of photography contests, on- and off-line.

Web Sites

Family photographs can provide great visuals for almost any homepage—including your own. Even if you don't take your pictures with a digital camera, you can purchase an inexpensive scanner, and turn your film images into digital files to use on your web page, or to e-mail to your friends and family.

Scrapbooks

A scrapbook is a great way to collect and organize your photos. Just make sure that all the materials you use in your scrapbook are acid free and labeled as safe for photos. Be especially careful about the adhesives you select. Photo corners are safe, as are some specially manufactured glues and tapes, but others can damage your photos over time. Scrapbooks don't have to include just special events or vacations—photos of your pets, your home, and everyday things (like summer days in the backyard) also help to preserve special memories.

Framing and Matting

With proper matting and framing, your photographs will be a source of pride and beauty for years to come. Whether you have them professionally matted and framed, or do it yourself, family photographs can bring life, color and fun to almost any room. The key to great framing and decorating success, starts with great photos. Once you have great images, your decorating choices are nearly limitless.

However you choose to share or exhibit your photos, you'll have more professional (and more enjoyable!) images when you use the compositional and lighting techniques you've learned in this book. Happy trails!

Glossary

ADVANCED PHOTO SYSTEM (APS). A camera and film photographic system that offers drop-in film cartridges, multiple print formats (including panoramic view), in-cartridge negative storage and other features.

APERTURE. The lens opening of the camera through which light passes to hit the film.

ASA. A film speed rating similar to ISO that indicates a film's sensitivity to light.

BULL'S-EYE EFFECT. Centering a photographic subject in the viewfinder, creating static, unappealing composition.

COLOR NEGATIVES. Processed color print film. The color negative is used to make a positive or color print.

COLOR PRINT FILM. Film that is used to create color prints.

COLOR TRANSPARENCY FILM. Positive images created on a transparent film base for projected viewing. This is also called color slide film.

COMPOSITION. The positioning of elements in a scene to create visual impact and to imply depth in a photograph.

DEPTH OF FIELD. The area of a photograph that is acceptably sharp or in focus. Three factors (lens focal length, camera-to-subject distance, and aperture) control how much depth of field is in a photograph.

DIGITAL CAMERAS. Cameras that use electronic information, rather than film, to record and store an image.

EXPOSURE CONTROLS. Camera settings, either automatic or manual, that allow light to expose the film through the camera's lens and shutter. The amount of light that reaches the film is controlled by the aperture and shutter speed. (*See also* Proper Exposure.)

FILM. The light-sensitive material used to record a photographic image.

FILM SPEED RATING. Film speed ratings (ISO or ASA) indicate a film's sensitivity to light and are expressed in numbers ranging from 25 to 3200. The higher the number, the less light required to adequately expose the film.

FOCAL LENGTH. A measurement (in millimeters) of a lens' ability to magnify a subject. The higher the number, the greater the magnification of the lens.

FOCUSING CONTROLS. Automatic or manual controls that allow the photographer to focus light through the lens onto the film in order to render a sharply focused subject.

FRAMING. A compositional technique that uses foreground objects in all or part of the scene to frame the subject and to create depth in the scene.

GOLDEN HOURS. The time of day (usually from dawn to about an hour after sun up; and from an hour before sunset to sunset) that creates dramatic and golden light. This light is ideal for most photographic endeavors.

GRAIN. In an enlarged image, the speckled or "grainy" look caused by the tiny particles of silver in a negative having been magnified to such a degree that they become visible.

HANDCOLORING. The process of applying, by brush or other method, color oils to a black & white photo.

ISO. A film speed rating similar to ASA that indicates a film's sensitivity to light.

LENS. A piece (or several pieces) of optical glass which focus the light from a scene onto the film.

LIGHT METER. An instrument that measures the amount of light in a scene. Light meters in cameras measure the amount of light reflected from a scene in order to make a proper exposure.

MACRO LENS. A special close-up lens that allows for focusing on objects at very close distances.

NORMAL LENS. A lens that sees an angle of view roughly what the human eye sees in a fixed position. For 35mm cameras, a normal lens is 50mm.

PERSPECTIVE. The apparent size of objects in a scene relative to each other.

PERSPECTIVE CONTROL. Using lenses and composition to affect the apparent size of objects in a scene.

POINT AND SHOOT. Compact, easy-to-use, automatic cameras.

PROPER EXPOSURE. The amount of light (controlled by the aperture and shutter speed) required to render a well exposed image (one that is neither too light, nor too dark).

RESOLUTION. The relative sharpness of a photograph or area of a photograph.

RULE OF THIRDS. A technique that divides the viewfinder into three equal parts vertically and horizontally to facilitate better photographic composition.

SHUTTER. The mechanism on a camera that opens and closes to expose the film.

SHUTTER SPEED. The amount of time the the shutter remains open and light is allowed to hit the film.

SINGLE USE CAMERAS. Preloaded, inexpensive cameras that are designed to be used once and discarded as part of the film processing. Also called disposable cameras. Some are specially designed for underwater use, or for taking panoramic photos.

SINGLE LENS REFLEX. A camera in which the image is viewed through the camera's lens. This is made possible by the use of a mirror and prism.

SUBJECT. The person or object that is the main focus of a photograph (the reason for taking the photo).

TELEPHOTO LENS. Any lens with a longer than "normal" focal length. For 35mm photography, any lens in which the focal length is greater than 50mm.

TONING. The process of changing the overall color (or tone) of a black & white photograph.

VIEWFINDER. The small window on a camera (other than SLR cameras) through which a subject is seen and composed.

WIDE ANGLE LENS. Any lens with a shorter than "normal" focal length. For 35mm photography, any lens in which the focal length is less than 50mm.

ZOOM LENS. A lens that is adjustable to a range of focal lengths, often from wide angle to telephoto.

HINTS & TIPS

For more information on photographic techniques, consult one of the many books published by Amherst Media, Inc., which span an extensive number of topics (www.AmherstMedia.com). In addition, using various search engines, you can search by photographic subjects on the Internet for information on cameras, film, photographic accessories, handcoloring, and other subjects. Sites such as www.iwon.com; www.yahoo.com; www.dogpile.com; and www.metacrawler.com are good places to start your search. Canon, Nikon, Olympus, Minolta, Contax, Pentax, Kodak, Fuji, Ilford, Agfa, and other companies all have Internet home pages with up-to-the minute information on their specific camera and film products.

Index

Other Books from
Amherst Media

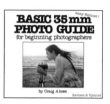

Basic 35mm Photo Guide, 5th Edition
Craig Alesse

Great for beginning photographers! Designed to teach 35mm basics step-by-step—completely illustrated. Features the latest cameras. Includes: 35mm automatic, semi-automatic cameras, camera handling, ƒ-stops, shutter speeds, and more! $12.95 list, 9x8, 112p, 178 photos, order no. 1051.

Beginner's Guide to Digital Imaging
Rob Sheppard

Learn how to select and use digital technologies that will lend excitement and provide increased control over your images—whether you prefer digital capture or film photography. $29.95 list, 8½x11, 128p, 80 full-color photos, order no. 1738.

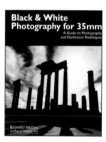

Black & White Photography for 35mm
Richard Mizdal

A guide to shooting and darkroom techniques! Perfect for beginning or intermediate photographers who want to improve their skills. Features helpful illustrations and exercises to make every concept clear and easy to follow. $29.95 list, 8½x11, 128p, 100+ b&w photos, order no. 1670.

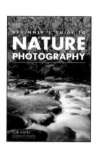

Beginner's Guide to Nature Photography
Cub Kahn

Whether you prefer a walk through a neighborhood park or a hike through the wilderness, the beauty of nature is ever present. Learn to create images that capture the scene as you remember it with the simple techniques found in this book. $14.95 list, 6x9, 96p, 70 full-color photos, order no. 1745.

How to Take Great Pet Pictures
Ron Nichols

From selecting film and equipment to delving into animal behavior, Nichols teaches all that beginners need to know to take well-composed, well-exposed photos of these "family members" that will be cherished for years. $14.95 list, 6x9, 80p, 40 full-color photos, order no. 1729.

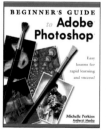

Beginner's Guide to Adobe® Photoshop®
Michelle Perkins

Learn the skills you need to make your images look their best, create original artwork or add unique effects to any image. All topics are presented in short, easy-to-digest sections that will boost confidence and ensure outstanding images. $29.95 list, 8½x11, 128p, 150 full-color photos, order no. 1732.

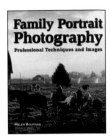

Family Portrait Photography

Helen Boursier

Learn from professionals how to operate a successful portrait studio. Includes: marketing family portraits, advertising, working with clients, posing, lighting, and selection of equipment. Includes images from a variety of top portrait shooters. $29.95 list, 8½x11, 120p, 123 photos, index, order no. 1629.

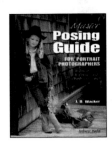

Master Posing Guide for Portrait Photographers

J. D. Wacker

Learn the techniques you need to pose single portrait subjects, couples and groups for studio or location portraits. Includes techniques for photo-graphing weddings, teams, children, special events and much more. $29.95 list, 8½x11, 128p, 80 photos, order no. 1722.

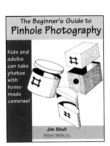

The Beginner's Guide to Pinhole Photography

Jim Shull

Take pictures with a camera you make from stuff you have around the house. Develop and print the results at home! Pinhole photography is fun, inexpensive, educational and challenging. $17.95 list, 8½x11, 80p, 55 photos, charts & diagrams, order no. 1578.

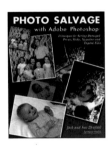

Photo Salvage with Adobe® Photoshop®

Jack and Sue Drafahl

This indispensible book will teach you how to digitally restore faded images, correct exposure and color balance problems and processing errors, eliminate scratches and much, much more. $29.95 list, 8½x11, 128p, 200 full-color photos, order no. 1751.

More Photo Books Are Available

Contact us for a FREE catalog:

Amherst Media, PO Box 586, Amherst, NY 14226 USA

www.AmherstMedia.com

Ordering & Sales Information:

INDIVIDUALS: If possible, purchase books from an Amherst Media retailer. Write to us for the dealer nearest you. To order direct, send a check or money order with a note listing the books you want and your shipping address. For U.S. delivery, freight charges for first book are $4.00 (add $1.00 for each additional book). For delivery to Canada/Mexico, freight charges for first book are $9.00 (add $2.50 for each additional book). For delivery to all other countries, freight charges for first book are $11.00 (add $2.50 for each additional book). Visa and MasterCard accepted. New York state residents add 8% sales tax.

DEALERS, DISTRIBUTORS & COLLEGES: Write, call or fax to place orders. For price information, contact Amherst Media or an Amherst Media sales representative. Net 30 days.

1(800)622-3278 or (716)874-4450, Fax: (716)874-4508,
All prices, publication dates, and specifications are subject to change without notice.
Prices are in U.S. dollars. Payment in U.S. funds only.